THE LITTLE BOOK BOOK FOR INTROVERTS

STRATEGIES, EXCUSES, AND COMFORTS FOR NON-PEOPLE PEOPLE

ROBB PEARLMAN

First published in the United States of America in 2024 by
Rizzoli Universe
A Division of Rizzoli International Publications, Inc.
300 Park Avenue South
New York, NY 10010
www.rizzoliusa.com

Publisher: Charles Miers
Associate Publisher: Jessica Fuller
Assistant Editor: Kate Avino
Design: Celina Carvalho
Production Manager: Colin Hough-Trapp

Printed in China

2024 2025 2026 2027 / 10 9 8 7 6 5 4 3 2 1

ISBN: 978-0-7893-4555-4
Library of Congress Control Number: 2024931511

Visit us online:
Facebook.com/RizzoliNewYork
Twitter: @Rizzoli_Books
Instagram.com/RizzoliBooks
Pinterest.com/RizzoliBooks
Youtube.com/user/RizzoliNY
Issuu.com/Rizzoli

TABLE OF CONTENTS

> "YOU NEED TO BE ALONE TO FIND OUT ANYTHING."
>
> VIVIENNE WESTWOOD

" THERE ARE JUST SOME TIMES YOU HAVE TO GIVE YOURSELF SPACE TO BE QUIET... "

MICHELLE OBAMA

A QUIET PLACE

For years, society has been telling introverts, in subtle and not-so-subtle ways, that we need to put the book down and come out of our shells, that we need to change the way we behave in public to succeed, that FOMO is somehow a real thing and not a marketing ploy created by liquor distributors and entertainment space owners, or that if we're alone we're necessarily lonely. To society I say: nope.

There is nothing wrong with being an introvert. There is something wrong, though, with thinking it's ok to tell an introvert that there's something wrong with them. Will an introvert miss out on something by not surrounding themselves with people and events? Sure, probably about as many things as an extrovert does by not appreciating their own company and creating their own experiences. Maybe, just maybe, society rarely hears anyone brag about the joys of being an introvert because extroverts have been talking—oh so very loudly— over them.

So put down that self-help book that's telling you to get out of the house more, walk away from that seminar that insists that the only way to get ahead at work is to go out drinking with your coworkers, and shut off the (probably soon-to-be-canceled) comedian's special before he makes you think that needing to recharge your internal batteries is, somehow, laughable.

This book celebrates the countless joys of being an introvert. You, quiet reader, will find spaces to contribute your own ideas, stickers to signal your often unspoken and inner thoughts, a myriad of excuses to get out of obligations, and, hopefully, enough fodder to keep extroverts in their place and out of yours.

READING IS FUNDAMENTAL(LY ALL INTROVERTS WANT TO DO)

Most introverts are never more than an arm's length away from reading materials. It goes without saying that few introverts have the physical or psychological strength to pass a bookstore without stopping in for a "quick look around." And while this may be good news for shop owners and the local economy, it is bad news for anyone accompanying or waiting for them who believes that they literally mean it will be quick. It also often means that bedside tables must be built strong enough to accommodate towering "to be read" piles, and most wall space be appropriated for bookshelves.

Books allow readers, but especially introverted readers, a way to connect with authors, their fictional characters, or non-fiction subjects without having to actually interact with them. Unlike films or shows that can be put on in the background as ambient noise, books require at least a modicum of concentration to be enjoyed. So, when anyone picks up a book to read, their focus and energy shifts from taking in the world around them and onto and into processing whatever world—of their choice—that they're reading about. And while authors may control the narrative, readers are fully in control of the way they experience it.

It's no question that apps, eBooks, and audio books certainly make on-the-go reading a bit more convenient (and easier on the backs and shoulders), and they make it easier for introverts to enjoy reading in public. Whether it's enjoying a drink in a hotel bar after a long day, eating a meal at a local restaurant, or commuting on your way to or from the office, reading is as much a way of being in the world without having to necessarily interact with it, as it is the perfect way to pass the time. Unfortunately, many people see the book someone is reading as some sort of conversation-starter prop. Allow me to state, in certain terms, that this is not the case. Introverts (and, let's face it, anyone who's reading something) will unanimously agree that unless you are a waiter, bartender, or other service professional, a first responder, or our mother, the book we're holding is a barrier, not an invitation, to chat.

For those struggling, we've included some stickers that are perfect for placing on the cover of any book—to dissuade any (and by that we mean *all*) persons who try to engage in usually pointless, but always distracting, conversation.

THE BUDDY SYSTEM

It's a common misconception that introverts don't like anyone. That's not true. We don't like *everyone*. Which is a big difference.

In much the same way as the "Who Rescued Who" bumper sticker proposes that a pet parent has benefited more from the relationship than their adoptive pet has, or how a mentor/mentee program enriches the lives of their participants in equal measure, introverts and extroverts often share a particularly unique symbiotic relationship.

Introverts will often be found floundering in the wild, or by chance or circumstance, by an extrovert or select group of extroverts. After each party has the opportunity to size one another up, they'll be comfortable enough to be their authentic selves.

Introverts like being invited to things by their extroverts, but they love knowing that they can decline an invitation and not worry about not ever being invited again. They appreciate their extrovert's ability to raise their energy levels without exceeding their maximum capacity.

And perhaps most importantly, they truly value the fact that their extrovert can read secret physical and psychological signals from across the room, know when they've had enough, and, like Chris Hemsworth saving a kidnapped child from an international crime lord, extract them from any social situation.

Extroverts, for their part, appreciate the fact that their introverted friends don't go out all the time, which makes the time they do spend together all the more special. Extroverts like not having the pressure of constantly talking, moving, or otherwise expending energy with another person. Extroverts feel emotionally supported by their introvert's heightened ability to actively listen to their worries, concerns, and stories, and provide a calm and measured perspective. They also appreciate the way an introvert can cut through all of the noise, see the real them, and value a friendship.

Show me an introvert and I'll show you their extroverted friend. And, maybe, the one selfie they took together. But it'll be a good one!

GIVE ME OFFICE SPACE

Despite their enormous rise in popularity among introverted and extroverted employees, not every company offers work-from-home or hybrid models to their workers. Contrary to popular belief, the physical office space—that capitalistic bastion of harsh overhead lighting, sub-zero temperatures, performative corporate "culture," and packed-into-conference-room meetings that could have been an email—can actually be a haven for professional introverts and introverted professionals.

With office spaces being reconfigured and downsized, many companies are shifting toward open office floor plans. Free of most walls and private space and dotted with "quiet" telephone rooms or communal spaces to encourage the kind of teamwork and spontaneous idea-generating that employers always expect of their workers but never reward them for, open office floor plans are basically the design aesthetic of at least four of the nine circles of hell (the third circle is most likely filled with office pantries crammed with vending machines that only accept crisp new $2 bills). While extroverts may find themselves compelled to interact with everyone around them, introverts have years, if not decades, of experience blocking out unwarranted distraction and noise and concentrating at what's in front of them. And though it's easy to bristle at the lack of privacy that comes from sitting shoulder-to-shoulder with coworkers, any introvert with a set of headphones and good peripheral vision can enjoy observing all the office melodramas unfolding around them without ever having to actively participate in it. Hear that? Jenny from accounts payable is talking about Mary from accounts receivable again. Sorry, Audrey from HR, I haven't seen Jon. Oh boy, Russell keeps stealing the candy from Michelle's bowl. Did Ethan from marketing just break up with Don from publicity?

BATTERY: LOW

Everyone has a social battery. Introverts' batteries just happen to have different run times. These tips and tricks may help improve your charge time.

THE GREAT ESCAPE

The first step toward recharging is removing yourself from the situation that's draining you. While extroverts linger and engage in long-winded farewells, introverts have already slipped away, leaving only their polite smile as a hostess gift.

THE BLANKET BURRITO

Once at home, the "Blanket Burrito" is a classic way to recharge—especially when combined with the nacho recipe on page 15. Imagine cocooning yourself in layers of soft blankets, with only your eyes peeking out to watch your favorite show. The Blanket Burrito allows you to find layers of warmth and comfort in the familiar feel of home.

I LAND IN THE STREAMING SERVICES

Binging isn't necessarily just about watching TV; it's about getting lost in it. Whether it's watching an entire season of your favorite show for the third time, a brand-new movie, trying out K-dramas, or learning something about another evil billionaire from an intriguing documentary, screens become an introvert's portal to a realm of entertainment and escapism.

THE PET PARADOX

Often, the only living creatures introverts have patience for are their pets. Be it a cat, dog, turtle, bird, or potbellied pig, these companions offer comfort without the need for conversation. The mere act of petting an animal's fur or watching them play can be incredibly soothing. And if you're on your walk, you can use the time it takes for your dog to find just the right spot to contemplate your place in the world.

IT'S MURDER OUT THERE

The recent popularity of true crime podcasts offers introverts an opportunity to experience acceptable levels of anxiety, as well as the deep satisfaction that comes when a mystery is solved. It also provides introverts with plenty of reasons to not ever leave the house again.

YOU'LL BE ALL WRITE

Many introverts find writing, drawing, or journaling to be an excellent way to process social interactions and reflect on the day. By putting their thoughts on paper, introverts can creatively interpret and/or reinterpret their experiences and write new ones.

COLOR ME INTROVERTED

Coloring books are a wonderful representation of an introvert's predilection of being creative and experiential, while remaining within acceptable or known limits. They provide a great way to focus attention away from your day and toward recentering yourself. Note that you may find yourself using an inordinate amount of red if you color while listening to those murder podcasts, so adjust your shopping lists for colored pencils, markers, or crayons accordingly.

IN YOUR SPACE, NO ONE CAN HEAR YOU . . .

Like how Superman gets replenished by the rays of Earth's yellow sun, sometimes just sitting in utter silence, soaking up the tranquility of an empty room, can set an introvert on their way toward recharging. It can be like floating in a spaceship of solitude, exploring the galaxy of your thoughts without any external interference or fleeing from an exploding planet (note that you're on the exploding planet and there's no escape).

. . . SCREAM

Sometimes an introvert just needs to unleash their frustrations, annoyances, and social exhaustion into a pillow, letting out a muffled scream worthy of the most dramatic telenovelas. It's a cathartic release, a way to expel the pent-up energy from dealing with your day, and may serve as a muffled, yet clear, signal to those you live with to give you a few minutes to yourself.

COMFORT FOOD

No one sees the bright-orange, cheese-puff-colored line between gluttony and an enjoyably appetizing (if not always nutritious) experience like an introvert.

Whether used to satiate hunger, refuel, or even just as a snacky way to enhance an activity or just pass the time, food is never more delicious to an introvert than when it's enjoyed on their own terms. And in stretchy pants. These tried-and-true "recipes" offer viable, judgment-free serving suggestions for home and professional chefs alike.

COFFEE OR TEA

If anyone asks you how you take your coffee or tea, tell them "with silence." This popular beverage is the perfect thing to enjoy alone, with friends and loved ones, at home or in public.

INGREDIENTS:

The beverage of your choice

If at home:
Your favorite mug, cup, or tumbler

If in public:
Headphones
Reusable tumbler or mug
A book, computer, tablet, or something to look at

DIRECTIONS FOR HOME:

1. Prepare whatever beverage you and your friends or loved ones like.

2. Enjoy while talking, playing a game, watching TV, reading, in quiet contemplation, conversation, or however you like.

DIRECTIONS FOR BEING IN PUBLIC:

1. Bring your personal mug, cup, or tumbler to your favorite coffee shop.

2. Pass the vessel to the barista or counterperson and order your beverage.

3. While waiting for your order, scout a spot to sit. If you're alone you may prefer to face a wall so the barista isn't distracted, and you can avoid any unwarranted or unnecessary eye-to-eye contact with passersby or other customers.

4. Take your order to your table.

5. Place your headphones in your ears—even if you're not listening to music, and set up your book, computer, or tablet. All this may dissuade anyone who you didn't come with from talking to you.

OATMEAL

After a day of having Extroverts drain their internal reserves,
Introverts often need time to nourish their core,
shore up their foundation, or otherwise center themselves.
A hot bowl of carbohydrate-filled oatmeal will not only fill your belly
and replenish your energy, but will also go a long way toward filling
the existential void you've accumulated during the day.

INGREDIENTS:

Oats:
Choose your preferred type of oats. Old-fashioned rolled oats offer a hearty texture, while quick oats cook faster and have a smoother consistency.

Liquid:
You can use water or milk (dairy or non-dairy) to cook your oats. The choice depends on your preference for creaminess and flavor, and the amount of acid reflux or other gut issues you're suffering from as a result of forced interaction.

Sweetener:
Nutritionists may suggest you opt for a natural sweetener like honey or maple syrup, but feel free to use sugar, brown sugar, or even chocolate chips.

Toppings:
Customize your oatmeal with a variety of toppings such as fresh or dried fruits (bananas, berries, or apple slices), nuts (almonds, walnuts, or pecans), cinnamon or nutmeg, peanut or nut butter, or even your favorite protein powder.

DIRECTIONS:

If you're in a rush, you can certainly cook your oatmeal in a microwave. But you may find the slower, more gradual process required for stovetop cooking provides a much more relaxed, focused, and satisfying experience.

1. **Measure Your Oats:**
   Begin with a 1:2 ratio. For every 1/2 cup of oats, use 1 cup of your chosen liquid. As an easy reminder of the proportion, remember that you require 2 hours of recovery time for every 1 hour spent with people.

2. **Combine Oats and Liquid:**
   In a nonstick saucepan, combine your oats and liquid. Stir well to ensure the oats are evenly moistened.

3. **Heat the Mixture:**
   Place the saucepan over medium heat and bring the mixture to a gentle simmer. Stir occasionally to prevent sticking.

4. **Sweeten or Flavor to Taste:**
   Once the oats start to thicken (about 5-7 minutes), add your preferred sweetener, protein powder, or spices. Stir until they are fully dissolved. You might want to incorporate the peanut or nut butter at this time, so it softens enough to be fully incorporated.

5. **Customize with Toppings:**
   Transfer your cooked oatmeal to your favorite bowl or large mug and add whatever fresh fruits and nuts you like.

BUTTERED TOAST

More than just a staple from childhood sick days or as a breakfast side,
a plate of buttered toast can be enjoyed as a snack, side dish, or main
meal, a plate of buttered toast is as simple as it is simply satisfying.
And, if you're using store-bought sliced bread, easy enough
to make for a quiet shared meal with a trusted companion.

INGREDIENTS:

Bread

Butter

Jelly, jam, preserves, honey, nut butter, or cinnamon (optional)

DIRECTIONS:

1. **Remove Butter from Refrigerator:**
   Just as you need some time to decompress after a full day of being
   chilled by other people, your butter will need some time to come to room
   temperature. Give your butter as much time to soften as you yourself
   need, and you'll both be ready to spread on toast or the couch at the
   same time.

2. **Select Your Bread:**
   When choosing the foundation upon which to build your experience,
   consider your mood and preference. A hearty wheat or whole grain
   might be just healthy enough to counteract any amount of whole fat
   butter you'll be slathering upon it. A baguette could offer a touch of
   international elegance. A simple white bread could offer a blank enough
   canvas to add your toppings.

3. **Toast Your Bread:**

   In much the same way you may only be able to handle a few people at a time, your toaster, toaster oven, air fryer, or oven may not be able to accommodate a large number of slices. So in order to have it all come out hot-and-toasty, consider both the amount of bread you're intending to toast, as well as your desired level of toastiness. Whether you prefer it lightly golden, deep brown, or charred enough to burn away the last vestiges of human interaction you were subject to, this step should cater to your personal taste.

4. **Butter Your Toast:**

   Allow your toast to cool just enough to handle with your fingers. At this point, your butter should be relatively spreadable. Though you may relate to Bilbo Baggins, who famously felt as if he had been scraped too thin over too much toast, remember that the age of Hobbits and Elves has passed, so spread as much butter onto your toast as you like.

5. **Customize Your Moment:**

   Feel free to either savor the simplicity of your creation as it is, or add any complementary toppings as suits your taste.

NACHOS

Unlike Extroverts whose every thought, emotion, and interest can be seen on their surface, the ideas, feelings, and passions of Introverts are as layered, varied, and complex as a plate of nachos.

INGREDIENTS:

Tortilla Chips: Whether they're traditional, multigrain, gluten-free, or even flavored, tortilla chips serve as the foundation of your nachos, so make sure they're hearty enough to hold some weight, but not too flavored as to overpower the toppings.

Cheese: Shredded sharp cheddar, Monterey Jack, or a blend of the two melt well, but don't underestimate a processed cheese "product" for its ability to provide a flavorful, gooey, melty layer.

Protein (Optional): There's no reason a plate of nachos can't be a whole meal, so consider adding cooked and seasoned ground beef, shredded chicken, meat or vegetarian chili, black or refried beans to make it a well-balanced meal.

Toppings: Sliced jalapeños, grilled peppers, roasted garlic, diced tomatoes, black olives, finely chopped onions are classic options, but you can also add chili powder, sour cream, guacamole, salsa, or even a sprinkle of paprika, cumin, or cilantro all add depths of flavor.

DIRECTIONS:

1. **Preheat Your Oven** to 350°F (175°C). This will ensure your nachos are heated evenly and your cheese melts to perfection.

2. **Layer Your Chips:** On an oven-safe plate or baking sheet, arrange a layer of tortilla chips. Make sure they're evenly spread, so each chip gets its fair share of toppings.

3. **Add Cheese:** Pretend for a moment you're an extrovert spreading their unsolicited opinions on everyone and spread a generous amount of your chosen cheese or cheeses over the chips.

4. **Layer on the Protein (if desired):** If you're adding protein, evenly distribute it over the cheese-covered chips.

5. **Customize with Toppings:** Add any of the toppings (except for the ones that should be eaten cold or at room temperature, like salsa, guacamole, sour cream).

CHEESE PLATE

Nothing says comfort like cheese, especially when
it's eaten without anyone around to judge you
(including and especially your gastroenterologist
if you're lactose intolerant).

INGREDIENTS:

Assorted Cheeses: Whether it's grabbing something on the go, adding to
a salad or burger, or just eating over the sink at 2 a.m., it's always good to
have a wide variety of cheeses on hand. If you're planning something a little
more structured for watching a movie or show, you might want to choose a
cheese based on what you're watching as much as their textures and flavor
profiles. Aim to always place three to five types at a minimum, in your cart,
but only stop when you think the cheese monger or cashier will start to look
at you funny. Then add one more.

For dramas, select flavors that can match the intensity and complexity of
the storyline.

Aged Cheddar: More than just a throwback to the Lunchables of your
youth, the robust and sharp flavors of aged cheddar can mirror the depth of
emotions often found in dramatic narratives.
Its complexity can complement the layers of a well-crafted drama.

Gorgonzola: The bold and tangy profile of gorgonzola cheese can add
a touch of intensity to your cheese plate. It's a great option for shows or
movies that evoke strong emotions.

Manchego: The nutty and slightly salty taste of Manchego can provide a
rich and full-bodied flavor that complements the depth of a drama.

Parmigiano-Reggiano: With its savory and umami-rich characteristics, Parmigiano-Reggiano can add depth to your cheese plate. It's a great choice for stories that unfold over time.

Blue Cheese: Blue cheese, such as Roquefort or Stilton, offers a pungent and complex taste. It can bring a layer of complexity that mirrors the intricate plots often seen in dramas. Plus, it's fun to say "Bleu Cheese" in a French accent every time you take a bite.

Camembert: The creamy and earthy notes of Camembert can provide a sense of comfort that contrasts with the emotional intensity of a drama.

Smoked Gouda: Smoked gouda adds a smoky and slightly sweet flavor that can add depth and a touch of intrigue to your cheese plate, aligning with the mood of a drama.

Aged Gruyère: The nutty and caramelized flavors of aged Gruyère can offer a richness that pairs well with the emotional depth of a drama and can feel more comforting than a hug from any human being.

For comedies, consider flavors that can enhance the experience without overpowering the light-hearted and often whimsical nature of the content.

Mild Cheddar: A classic mild cheddar is a versatile option that pairs well with various types of comedy. Its creamy and slightly nutty flavor won't overwhelm your palate, allowing you to focus on the humor and less on the sandwich offerings in your office's vending machine.

Fresh Goat Cheese: The tangy and creamy profile of goat cheese offers a delightful contrast. It's light and refreshing, making it a great choice for comedies that leave you with a smile on your face.

Havarti: Havarti cheese is known for its buttery and slightly sweet taste. It's a gentle cheese that complements the light-hearted nature of comedies without stealing the spotlight.

Brie: The velvety texture and subtle earthiness of brie can provide an elegant touch to your comedy viewing experience. Like its namesake, it's a great option for shows or movies that have a touch of sophistication in their humor, like *Marvel Studio's Captain Marvel* rather than gritty dramas like *Room*.

Gouda: Gouda's slightly nutty and caramel-like notes can add depth to your cheese plate without overwhelming the comedy's atmosphere. Opt for a young gouda for a milder flavor.

Edam: Edam cheese is known for its mild and slightly salty taste. It's a good option for comedies where you want a cheese that's unassuming and easy to enjoy.

Monterey Jack: This cheese's mild and creamy profile makes it a crowd-pleaser. It's a safe choice that won't distract from the comedy on screen and may prompt you to rethink your assessment of some other supporting Disney characters.

Cheese Curds: For a fun and playful twist, consider including cheese curds. These bite-sized cheese pieces are a popular snack and can add a touch of whimsy to your cheese plate. And if anyone asks, you can say you were introduced to this main ingredient of poutine by your Canadian boyfriend who totally exists.

Crackers and Bread: Choose a selection of crackers, crisps, and bread. Think about textures here as well—some should be sturdy enough to hold the cheese, while others can be more delicate. Regardless, remember that carbs only count if they're in a sandwich or pasta, so go for it.

Charcuterie (Optional): For those who enjoy some savory meats, add slices of prosciutto, salami, or any other cured meats of your choice.

Fresh Fruit: Select a mix of fresh fruits like grapes, figs, and sliced apples or pears. These fruits add a touch of sweetness and balance the richness of the cheeses and, technically, make the whole thing a salad.

Nuts: Include a handful of your favorite nuts, such as almonds, walnuts, or cashews, for a satisfying crunch. Nuts are a good source of natural proteins and a way to keep people with nut allergies away from your cheese plate.

Honey, Jam, Mustard, Chutney, or Other Condiments: A drizzle of honey or a dollop of fruit jam pairs wonderfully with cheese and adds an extra layer of flavor.

DIRECTIONS:

1. Take the cheese out of the fridge and let it come to room temperature.

2. Put on elastic-waisted or other non-binding pants.

3. Cut the hard cheeses in slices or bite-sized cubes, leave the semi-soft ones in wedges, and place any soft ones in their container or transfer them to a bowl or individual plate to keep them from getting everywhere.

4. Arrange each of the elements. You should feel empowered to organize everything to your own preference, but I find that organizing each component on their own allows for a sense of endless variety as you assemble an endless amount of combinations. This also affords you the opportunity to spread out, buffet-style, rather than having everything confined to one large platter.

5. Place cheeses on a plate, serving platter, TV table, or lap desk. Scatter the fruit around the plate. This will make it look pretty and keep the cheeses from intermingling.

6. Place the crackers and bread in their own basket. This will keep the crumbs, or at least the ones that don't fall between your couch cushions or down the front of your shirt, all in one easy-to-empty spot.

7. Place the nuts in their own bowl.

8. Rather than transferring the condiments into their own individual bowls, simply place them, in their original containers, on a plate. This will save you time during clean up.

9. Place the optional Charcuterie selection on its own plate.

10. Savor each bite. Let the flavors mingle on your palate as you immerse yourself in whatever you're watching, binging, or have on while you're scrolling on your phone.

" LIFE WOULD BE WONDERFUL IF PEOPLE WOULD LEAVE YOU ALONE. "

CHARLIE CHAPLIN

POPCORN

Popcorn has long—and rightfully—been heralded by the movie industry
as the go-to treat for theaters across the globe.
But for those of us who'd rather not eat in a crowd, watch
a movie in a crowd, or do anything crowd-related,
popcorn offers everyone, but especially introverts, a unique
and seldom-spoken-of, hands-free snacking opportunity.

INGREDIENTS:

Popcorn

Butter (more than would be considered healthy, optional)

Dried Seasonings such as Salt, Pepper, Green Goddess,
Everything Bagel, Cheese, Ranch (optional)

DIRECTIONS:

1. Melt the butter in a saucepan or in the microwave.

2. Prepare popcorn as you normally would (or just open a bag of your
   favorite pre-popped brand).

3. Drizzle the butter on top.

4. Place 1/3 of the popcorn in a bowl and drizzle some of the butter and
   seasonings. Repeat 2 more times until all the popcorn is in the bowl.

5. Pick up a book, newspaper, phone, or whatever in your hand or hands.

6. Without taking your eyes or attention off what you're reading or looking at, slowly lower your face to the bowl and extend your tongue. The popcorn will magically stick to your tongue.

7. Return to your original position. Chew on the popcorn.

8. Repeat until you're done without ever having to put your book down!

PIZZA

There are thousands of reasons why pizza is the perfect food. But for introverts, they include the fact that it can be purchased, frozen, and kept in your freezer until you need it, it can be ordered and paid for online, cooked by someone else, and delivered fresh, piping-hot, and customized to your liking (and even left at your doorstep so you don't have to talk to the delivery person), and can then be eaten hot, or cold, for breakfast, lunch, dinner, or snacks, for days after, further minimizing the reasons to deal with anyone outside of your home.

So bookmark the website of your favorite family-owned pizzeria or chain, add them as a contact in your phone (for someone else to call), buy a dedicated freezer to stockpile your favorite store-bought brands, and give silent, but sincere thanks to the country of Italy for allowing you the opportunity to enjoy delicious and nutritious meals alone or with trusted and loved ones.

HALLOWEEN CANDY

**Just because you're an adult doesn't mean you
don't deserve a treat. Especially after you've been tricked
into answering the door.**

DIRECTIONS:

1. Buy a bag of fun-size Halloween candy. The kind you and whomever you live with like the best.

2. Steel yourself to receive trick-or-treaters from 2 to 6 p.m. Compliment the children on their costumes, and avoid eye contact with the adults if you can.

3. Lower your shades, close your drapes, shut off your porch light, or otherwise indicate that you are no longer receiving callers.

4. Eat as much candy as you'd like, for as long as it lasts, until next Halloween.

> **THE GOOD AND THE WISE
> LEAD QUIET LIVES.**
>
> **EURIPIDES**

OFFICE PERKS

Introverts can often avoid or make the best of social gatherings. But unless you're self-employed or work from home, it can often be extraordinarily difficult to enjoy employer mandated parties, especially when you're trying to balance a plate of food, a business conversation with the CFO, and maintaining your sanity.

DIRECTIONS:

1. Bring your favorite reusable food containers into the office. Keep them in your desk, locker, or other personal space.

2. RSVP yes to the invitation to the conference room, breakroom, cafeteria, pantry, or corner of the open office plan.

3. Get to the designated meeting place as the food arrives or is first set up.

4. Fill your plate full of pizza, cake, or other benefit your employer provides in lieu of a living wage and return to your office or workspace.

5. Transfer the food to your containers and place in a bag in the company refrigerator.

6. Return to the party with your plate. Pretend you've just finished eating.

7. Talk to people—especially your boss—and, once you have had enough, say you must return to your office to take/make an important call/email.

8. At the end of the day, take the food home with you.

9. Eat the food at home.

10. Return to the office and once again store the washed containers in your workspace.

11. Repeat as necessary.

WHIPPED CREAM

Contrary to popular belief (and by that I mean the unsolicited opinions of Extroverts), Introverts can be as silly, juvenile, and ridiculous as anyone.

INGREDIENTS:

Whipped Cream (preferably in a can)

Delivery Systems (optional), including but not limited to cookies, pie, cake, or pudding

DIRECTIONS:

1. Buy several cans of whipped cream. With all of the new and flavored varieties on the market, feel free to collect a bunch to make a buffet.

2. Spray directly into your own mouth, or the mouths of friends and loved ones.

3. Laugh uncontrollably at the fact that, as an adult, you can do this without much consequence (unless you're lactose intolerant, diabetic, or prone to cavities).

4. Optional: Apply the whipped cream to whatever cookies, pies, cakes, or puddings you like. It's totally up to you. Feel free to apply and eat on or over a plate, over the sink, while sitting on your couch, lying in your bed, or driving in your car.

"

I'M AN INTROVERT... I LOVE BEING BY MYSELF, LOVE BEING OUTDOORS, LOVE TAKING A LONG WALK WITH MY DOGS AND LOOKING AT THE TREES, FLOWERS, THE SKY.

"

AUDREY HEPBURN

EXCUSES, EXCUSES!

Sometimes, the only thing more exhausting for an introvert than attending (or recharging after) a social gathering is trying to come up with an excuse to get out of one. Many non-introverts cannot fathom the idea that not everyone is infected with chronic FOMO. So, even though "No" is a complete sentence, and "I'd prefer not to" is a valid an excuse to not do something, they require detailed reasoning or a long, drawn-out story as to why someone would decline an invitation.

Today's extended, blended, and global modern family may truthfully provide enough "sick" grandmothers, but that excuse may still ring of falsity if it's overused. The following collection of off-ramps will steer you away from Party Town. Just be sure to use the spaces to write in whom you made the excuse to, and when, so you don't accidentally repeat the same ones too often to the same people.

EXCUSE	GIVEN TO	DATE
There's an angry squirrel outside.		/ /
I have to keep refreshing my browser to get Taylor Swift tickets.		/ /
I can't because of reasons.		/ /
I'd tell you why, but they'll hear me.		/ /
I'm about to level up.		/ /

EXCUSE	GIVEN TO	DATE
I have to wash my everything.		/ /
My grandmother died.		/ /
My other grandmother died.		/ /
My other other grandmother died (I have a complicated family)		/ /
I have an avocado that's about to ripen.		/ /
My dog is going through some things.		/ /
My cat won't let me.		/ /
I have homework that's decades late.		/ /
I have to file TPS reports early tomorrow morning.		/ /
I'm suffering from chronic JoMO.		/ /
I have a standing appointment to lie down.		/ /
The floor is lava, and I can't get off my couch.		/ /
My mom says I can't.		/ /
I have a night doctor's appointment.		/ /

EXCUSE	GIVEN TO	DATE
These shows are burning a hole in my watch list.		__/__/__
I've been placed in time-out.		__/__/__
I have to read all my books before the library fines me.		__/__/__
I need to update a Wikipedia page before someone else does.		__/__/__
My glasses! I can't see anything without my glasses!		__/__/__
My internal battery needs recharging.		__/__/__
I'm doom-scrolling.		__/__/__
My plants will miss me too much.		__/__/__
My door's locked.		__/__/__
I'm currently at one with the force.		__/__/__
The pizza delivery kid will worry if I'm not home.		__/__/__
I'm helping my dad figure out his new phone.		__/__/__
I'm in a staring contest with the spider who lives in the corner of the living room.		__/__/__

EXCUSE	GIVEN TO	DATE
I'm watching paint dry.		/ /
I need to get to the neighbor's bouncy house before their kids do.		/ /
I'm busy trying to figure out who took the cookie from the cookie jar.		/ /
I'm on X in the dictionary and won't sleep until I know how it ends.		/ /
Gandalf said I shall not pass.		/ /
My astrologer advises against it.		/ /
My Magic 8 Ball doesn't think it's a good idea.		/ /
I need to patch things up with my fish.		/ /
I'm in the middle of a ducking fight with autocorrect.		/ /
It's too close to the holiday season.		/ /
All of my "going out" clothes are in the wash.		/ /
I'm planning on screaming into the void at that time.		/ /
I'm expecting a call about extending my car's warranty.		/ /

EXCUSE	GIVEN TO	DATE
I'm helping my mom with her computer.		__ / __ / __
I have a candle burning.		__ / __ / __
I can't risk harming my perfect Uber rating.		__ / __ / __
Unfortunately, everything I like is here, not out there.		__ / __ / __
I'm boldly going nowhere.		__ / __ / __
They'll get me if I go outside.		__ / __ / __
My alien abduction is scheduled for tonight.		__ / __ / __
I'm lactose intolerant and ate too much cheese today.		__ / __ / __
The air quality report says it currently has too many people in it.		__ / __ / __
My bath bomb has just gone off.		__ / __ / __
I'm a backward vampire and can only go out in the daytime.		__ / __ / __
I'm busy reliving my childhood in the pillow fort I just built.		__ / __ / __
I just worked the butt groove into my couch cushions and can't leave it.		__ / __ / __

EXCUSE	GIVEN TO	DATE
I must obsessively track the status of an order.		___ / ___ / ___
I'm playing tag with my neighbor and must stay inside and out of reach.		___ / ___ / ___
I keep getting a sign to "stop," so I can't go any farther than the end of my street.		___ / ___ / ___
I plead the fifth.		___ / ___ / ___
I'm working on a podcast.		___ / ___ / ___
Oh, you know why.		___ / ___ / ___
I'm grounded.		___ / ___ / ___

" THERE'S NO SHAME IN LIVING A QUIET LIFE. "

DANIEL RADCLIFFE

BOOKS READ

As any librarian will attest, introverts have years of experience building, nurturing, and valuing their relationships with books. And though they've traded in "reading under the covers by flashlight" to "reading under a weighted blanket by clip-on booklight, so you don't wake your partner, and supported by a mountain of ergonomic pillows," the magic remains. Use the following space to record the books removed from your TBR pile.

TITLE	DATE FINISHED
	__ / __ / __
	__ / __ / __
	__ / __ / __
	__ / __ / __
	__ / __ / __
	__ / __ / __
	__ / __ / __
	__ / __ / __

TITLE	DATE FINISHED
	___ / ___ / ___
	___ / ___ / ___
	___ / ___ / ___
	___ / ___ / ___
	___ / ___ / ___
	___ / ___ / ___
	___ / ___ / ___
	___ / ___ / ___
	___ / ___ / ___
	___ / ___ / ___
	___ / ___ / ___
	___ / ___ / ___
	___ / ___ / ___
	___ / ___ / ___
	___ / ___ / ___

TITLE	DATE FINISHED
	___ / ___ / ___
	___ / ___ / ___
	___ / ___ / ___
	___ / ___ / ___
	___ / ___ / ___
	___ / ___ / ___
	___ / ___ / ___
	___ / ___ / ___
	___ / ___ / ___
	___ / ___ / ___
	___ / ___ / ___
	___ / ___ / ___
	___ / ___ / ___
	___ / ___ / ___
	___ / ___ / ___

TITLE	DATE FINISHED
	_____ / / _____
	_____ / / _____
	_____ / / _____
	_____ / / _____
	_____ / / _____
	_____ / / _____

> "
> **THERE'S A REALLY POSITIVE SIDE** OF BEING AN INTROVERT— YOU REALLY PICK UP ON THINGS **A LOT MORE THAN YOUR** EXTROVERTED COUNTERPARTS.
> "
> **JESSICA WILLIAMS**

FILMS/SHOWS WATCHED

Sometimes the sweetest words an introvert can encounter are "director's cut" or "all seasons now available." "Extended version" works, too, but that may lead to a sitcom-worthy double-entendre misunderstanding if it's combined with an invitation to "Stream and Chill"—because introverts may actually want to watch something. Use the following space to keep track of all of the films and shows you watch this year.

TITLE	DATE ADDED	DATE WATCHED
	___/___/___	___/___/___
	___/___/___	___/___/___
	___/___/___	___/___/___
	___/___/___	___/___/___
	___/___/___	___/___/___
	___/___/___	___/___/___
	___/___/___	___/___/___
	___/___/___	___/___/___
	___/___/___	___/___/___

TITLE	DATE ADDED	DATE WATCHED
	__ / / __	__ / / __
	__ / / __	__ / / __
	__ / / __	__ / / __
	__ / / __	__ / / __
	__ / / __	__ / / __
	__ / / __	__ / / __
	__ / / __	__ / / __
	__ / / __	__ / / __
	__ / / __	__ / / __
	__ / / __	__ / / __
	__ / / __	__ / / __
	__ / / __	__ / / __
	__ / / __	__ / / __
	__ / / __	__ / / __

TITLE	DATE ADDED	DATE WATCHED
	___/___/___	___/___/___
	___/___/___	___/___/___
	___/___/___	___/___/___
	___/___/___	___/___/___
	___/___/___	___/___/___
	___/___/___	___/___/___
	___/___/___	___/___/___
	___/___/___	___/___/___
	___/___/___	___/___/___
	___/___/___	___/___/___
	___/___/___	___/___/___
	___/___/___	___/___/___
	___/___/___	___/___/___
	___/___/___	___/___/___
	___/___/___	___/___/___

TITLE	DATE ADDED	DATE WATCHED
	___ / ___ / ___	___ / ___ / ___
	___ / ___ / ___	___ / ___ / ___
	___ / ___ / ___	___ / ___ / ___
	___ / ___ / ___	___ / ___ / ___
	___ / ___ / ___	___ / ___ / ___
	___ / ___ / ___	___ / ___ / ___

" I RESTORE MYSELF WHEN I'M ALONE. "

MARILYN MONROE

GAMES PLAYED

Introverts are not NPCs. They are as much active, fully engaged players in their own lives as they are in those of their families, friends, and coworkers. Whether playing alone, online, or in person, everyone can enjoy the escapism and comfort found within video games, RPGs, MMOs, tabletop games, and other gaming. Use the following space to record the time you spend adventuring.

TITLE	DATE COMPLETED	TOTAL HOURS PLAYED
	__ / __ / __	
	__ / __ / __	
	__ / __ / __	
	__ / __ / __	
	__ / __ / __	
	__ / __ / __	
	__ / __ / __	
	__ / __ / __	
	__ / __ / __	

TITLE	DATE COMPLETED	TOTAL HOURS PLAYED
	___ / ___ / ___	
	___ / ___ / ___	
	___ / ___ / ___	
	___ / ___ / ___	
	___ / ___ / ___	
	___ / ___ / ___	
	___ / ___ / ___	
	___ / ___ / ___	
	___ / ___ / ___	
	___ / ___ / ___	
	___ / ___ / ___	
	___ / ___ / ___	
	___ / ___ / ___	
	___ / ___ / ___	
	___ / ___ / ___	

TITLE	DATE COMPLETED	TOTAL HOURS PLAYED
	__ / __ / __	
	__ / __ / __	
	__ / __ / __	
	__ / __ / __	
	__ / __ / __	
	__ / __ / __	
	__ / __ / __	
	__ / __ / __	
	__ / __ / __	
	__ / __ / __	
	__ / __ / __	
	__ / __ / __	
	__ / __ / __	
	__ / __ / __	
	__ / __ / __	

TITLE	DATE COMPLETED	TOTAL HOURS PLAYED
	___ / / ___	
	___ / / ___	
	___ / / ___	
	___ / / ___	
	___ / / ___	

"SILENCE IS A SOURCE OF GREAT STRENGTH."

LAO TZU

"

BEING ALONE IS NOT THE SAME AS BEING LONELY.

"

TAYLOR SWIFT

EARPHONES IN=
Tuning Out

ALONE
and at Peace

I DON'T
want
to be
HERE

MY
SOCIAL
BATTERIES
ARE DRAINED

I Like
MY OWN
COMPANY

CAN'T YOU SEE I'M READING?

Homebody

I Don't Want to GO

NO, I DON'T WANT YOU TO JOIN ME

YES ✗ NO

At Home & At Peace

No,
I DON'T WANT
Company

I enjoy
my own
company

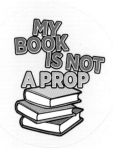

INTROVERTED

*But willing
to talk about*

_____

_____

INTROVERTED

*But willing
to talk about*

_____

_____

INTROVERTED

*But willing
to talk about*

_____

_____

INTROVERTED

*But willing
to talk about*

_____

_____

INTROVERTED

*But willing
to talk about*

_____

_____